SPRING 2019

IN THIS ISSUE:

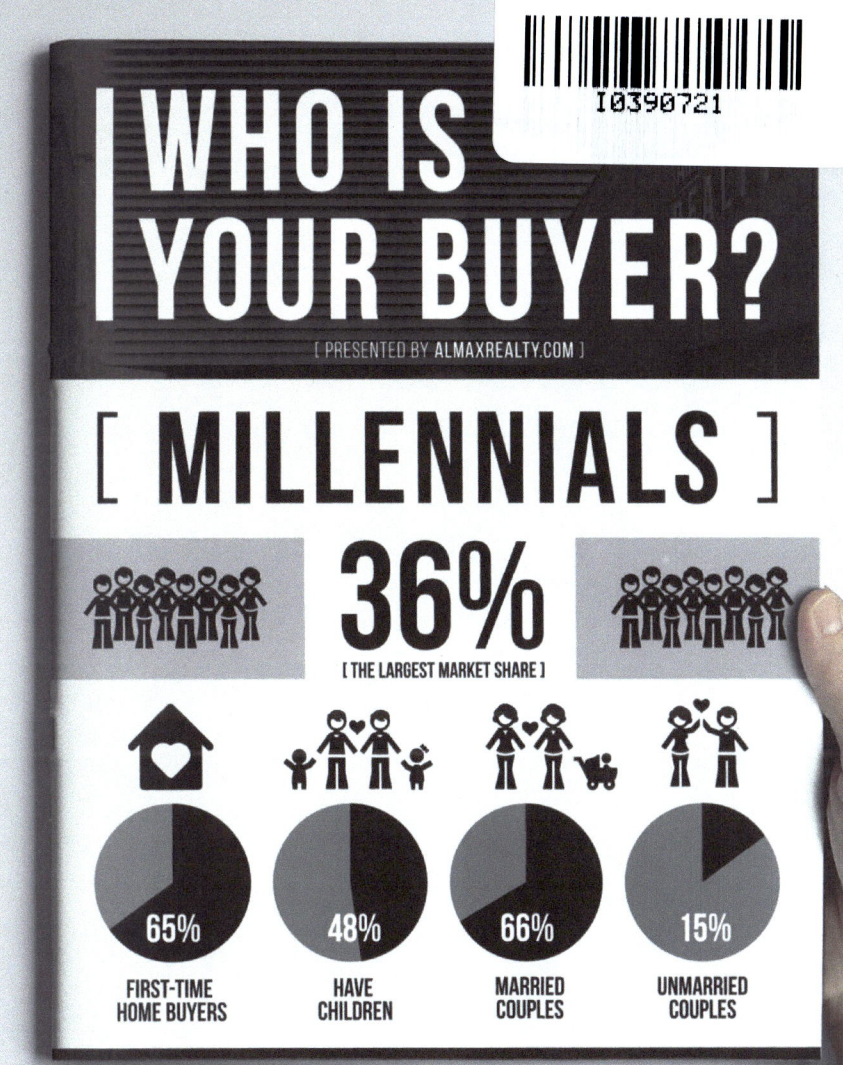

WHO IS YOUR BUYER?
[PRESENTED BY ALMAXREALTY.COM]

[MILLENNIALS]

36%
[THE LARGEST MARKET SHARE]

65%	48%	66%	15%
FIRST-TIME HOME BUYERS	HAVE CHILDREN	MARRIED COUPLES	UNMARRIED COUPLES

[2019 MARKET TRENDS]

| FROM THE EDITORS:

Wow, it's just the beginning of the year and there is so much to talk (and look) about!

In this issue we are introducing Duncan Avenue Group's brand new enterprise: Alexander Maxwell Realty and the latest home design project by Duncan Avenue Studio.

Thank you for getting a copy of the Hudson Valley Style Magazine! We appreciate your support!

Maxwell & Dino Alexander

HUDSON VALLEY STYLE MAGAZINE

© 2019 Hudson Valley Style Magazine
A Duncan Avenue Group Publication
Contact Us:
World/US: 1-845-518-2750
HudsonValley.Style

HUDSON VALLEY **STYLE** 1

ALEXANDER MAXWELL REALTY | UPGRADE YOUR REALITY™
MEET THE NEW KIND OF REALTY

DINO ALEXANDER
Principal Broker, Alexander Maxwell Realty

New York State Licensed Real Estate Broker and Chief Executive Officer at the Duncan Avenue Group, Dino is an Expert in Business and Economics and has a vast experience in real estate, high-end fashion, and retail industries. Dino believes that Hudson Valley has a unique role in the Global Economy and the Modern Rustic Hudson Valley Style represents it on a Global scale.

Alexander Maxwell Realty is not just a Team of Realtors, but also a family. We know that a happy family starts with a happy home. We love to help our clients to find a happy place while investing in their future.

MAXWELL ALEXANDER
N.Y.S. Licensed Real Estate Sales Person, Alexander Maxwell Realty

Designer, Creative Director, Editor-in-Chief of the Hudson Valley Style Magazine, and World Class Brand Strategist, Maxwell has elevated creative-, design- and cultural value for hundreds of brands all around the World, ranging from technology startups, wellness & fitness brands, to Fortune 500 companies and globally renown non-profit organizations and government agencies.

As a Licensed Real Estate Salesperson, experienced Real Estate Investor/Developer, and Chief Design Officer of the Duncan Avenue Group, Maxwell exclusively represents Authentic Hudson Valley™ properties designed by the Award-Winning Duncan Avenue Design Studio.

WHY LIST WITH #ALMAXREALTY?

When you choose Alexander Maxwell Realty you choose a company which helps to invest in your future, to us you are not a one-off client – we form long-standing relationships with all our valued customers. To us, your property is a work of art and it is exactly how our All-inclusive Strategic Marketing Package will present it to the World:

1. LET'S MEET AND BRAINSTORM

At our first meeting and walkthrough of your property, we will discuss the initial market assessment, pricing, and marketing strategy. We will talk about your goals and the best way to reach them. We'll help you to achieve an optimal market positioning based on your goals, whether it is the sale price or timing.

2. IT'S TIME FOR A FACELIFT

Whether it is a brand new construction or a 200-year-old castle, your property will get a facelift based on the Strategy we agreed upon at the first step. It could be as little as a few expert staging recommendations or even more extensive measures such as paint or landscape improvement. We'll show you the numbers and how a small tweak at the initial stage can deliver tremendous return at the closing. Our industry partners can get the job done timely and efficiently, we even provide easy financing options if necessary.

3. PR AND MARKETING GEARS ARE STARTING TO SPIN

Next, we will start executing the Strategy: whether it is an award-winning real estate photography, property branding, aerial/drone imaging, video walkthrough, social media campaign, search engines optimization, feature in a critically acclaimed publication with a global reach, or all of the above - it is all included in our Strategic Marketing Package at no additional cost to you!

4. HERE IS THE FUN PART!

When the listing is ready to be presented in all of its glory, we will hold the first open house event and invite potential buyers, real estate brokers, industry leaders, news outlets and members of the public. At the end of the event, we will distribute a press-release, interviews, and event photos through 250+ media/pr/news channels and push the property listing via MLS, Zillow, Realtor.com, Trulia and 100+ other real estate marketing platforms.

5. BUILDING WINDMILLS, NOT WALLS

Real Estate is a dynamic and ever-changing market. Those who can harness the energy of the winds of change will eventually win. During the time on the market, we will help you to negotiate offers and adjust your Strategy based on the market feedback.

6. PAPER-PUSHING IS STILL A THING, EVEN WHEN IT'S DIGITAL

Selling Real Estate is a process that involves many team players and an enormous workflow of documents. Our team will assist you and your legal team with paperwork all the way from the beginning until closing and we will stay on top of the timeline, making sure everything is on track!

STYLE, DESIGN, AND INTELLIGENCE SPEAK VOLUMES. WE FLY WITH EAGLES, SO SHOULD YOUR REAL ESTATE MARKETING CAMPAIGN. TAKE IT TO THE NEXT LEVEL WITH #ALMAXREALTY

#DUNCANAVENUE
#INTERIORDESIGN

A HISTORIC
HUDSON VALLEY HOME
REIMAGINED

COVER STORY & PHOTOGRAPHY
BY **MAXWELL ALEXANDER**

Welcome to the historic (circa 1870) home in the heart of the quaint Village of Cornwall on Hudson, NY. Completely reimagined by the award-winning Duncan Avenue Design Studio the home was transformed into architecturally inspiring yet energy efficient masterpiece. It was fully renovated with design, sustainability, functionality

and comfort in mind. Contemporary open concept floorplan and two-story-high foyer bring an abundance of light in the space. Wake up to the sunrise shining through double glass doors on the east side of the house and watch the warm sunset rays shining through plenty of energy-efficient windows on the west. High-end finishes such as hardwood floors in 2 bedrooms upstairs, pet-friendly waterproof recycled vinyl on the main level, sustainable concrete counter tops, wood kitchen cabinets, stainless steel appliances, and designer light fixtures are only a few of the updates along with a brand-new central air system controlled by smart Nest thermostat with two-zone sensors.

CONTEMPORARY
SMART
FLOOR PLAN

The home has been designed to feel open, bright and spacious. Two-story-high foyer welcomes and inspires you just upon entering the home, then it seamlessly flows into an open concept living space/ kitchen and dining area set up for entertainment and get-togethers. Front of the house features additional and brightly lit office space with an unobstructed view through an entire home all the way to the natural landscape on the back of the property. Energy Star equipped laundry is conveniently hidden behind custom-built

barn door on the main level of the home, right next to the guest restroom. Both bedrooms along with the main bathroom are located on the second floor equipped with intelligent energy-saving sensors controlling the comfort settings. Partially finished basement and attic provide plenty of storage space and hold HVAC and other mechanicals in the separate utility room. There is an exit from the basement to the back of the property through a covered workshop area tucked away under the deck.

THIS SPECTACULAR KITCHEN IS READY TO HOST A COOKING SHOW

The kitchen is the heart of any home and this modern rustic kitchen is a perfect playground for a seasoned cook or an aspiring YouTube cooking show host. It's not just the size of the kitchen, but also the contemporary and eco-conscious features that are also impressive.

CORNWALL LANDING

[HUDSON VALLEY STYLE INTERIOR DESIGN]

Materials ↓

LED Pendants →

↑ Paint Colors

← Stainless Steel Range Hood

← Recycled Marble Mosaic

Concrete Counters →

CONCRETE COUNTER TOPS

This kitchen has a lot of character thanks to the sophisticated/industrial look of concrete countertops. They are not just trendy, but also environmentally-friendly. One of the unique characteristics of concrete is that this material will evolve and adopt character over time, so the appearance of your counters will improve with age. Concrete counters are durable and heat-resistant for all of you avid bakers out there. The material is non-toxic, does not emit VOCs unlike plastics/polymers and is a sustainable material, unlike granite or marble. Concrete is a friend of the environment in all stages of its life span, from raw material production to demolition, making it a natural choice for sustainable home construction.

STAINLESS STEEL ENERGY STAR APPLIANCES

Stainless Steel Energy Star Appliances are an important accord in an overall symphony of this amazing and functional kitchen. They are positioned in the most efficient way to ensure an easy cooking process. The kitchen features range hood vented outside of the house and stylish yet environmentally-friendly electric range. Hudson Valley region energy providers offer an option to switch to 100% renewable electricity from wind and solar, so the electric range makes a lot of sense.

HARDWOOD CABINETRY AND FUNCTIONAL DECORATIVE FEATURES

Compared to other building materials, wood leaves a smaller carbon footprint. When trees are sustainably harvested and manufactured into products, they continue to store carbon and keep it out of the atmosphere. One-half of the dry-weight of wood is carbon, so every time wood is used in furniture and other renovation projects, it serves as a carbon repository as well.

CUSTOM-BUILT FLOATING VANITY AND BARN DOORS, CERAMIC TILE, DESIGNER LED LIGHT FIXTURES, AN ABUNDANCE OF LIGHT & STORAGE CREATE SPA-QUALITY EXPERIENCE. GUEST BATHROOM FEATURES UNIQUE DESIGN AS WELL.

HIGH-END MODERN RUSTIC BATHROOMS

#COMFORT
#EFFICIENCY
#FUNCTIONALITY

1ST FLOOR LAUNDRY HIDDEN BEHIND A BARN DOOR

**CABLE
RAILING
& LED
CHANDELIER**

[HUDSON VALLEY STYLE INTERIOR DESIGN]

BARN DOOR CLOSETS & BAMBOO FEATURE WALL IN THE MASTER BEDROOM

BRIGHT AND SPACIOUS OFFICE SPACE

#AUTHENTIC #HUDSONVALLEY #STYLE

#MODERN
#AUTHENTIC
#RUSTIC

[LEARN MORE AT DUNCANAVEN   M]

SELLING REAL ESTATE
#HUDSONVALLEYSTYLE

By Dino Alexander

(Principal Broker, Alexander Maxwell Realty)

Want to sell your home quickly and for top dollar? Staging in Style can help. Staging is presenting your home in its best and most appealing light to the majority of home-buyers.

In theory, staging isn't hard or costly, but in reality, many homeowners find it difficult because it's often hard to see something objectively when we love it.

An easy way to see effectively staged homes is to visit decorated models. Decorating a model is expensive, but builders are willing to invest the cost because they understand just how well a staged home sells. You too can profit from this knowledge.

Why do some sellers balk at staging their home? They think it's too expensive, they think it's too much work, they like their decorating, and they don't understand the value.

Expensive? Decorating with Style is not nearly as much as your first price reduction.

Work? Mostly cleaning and de-cluttering which you would have to do anyway since you're moving.

Decorating? Liking your decorating is understandable. Look at it this way – interior design is for living in your home, staging is for selling your home. They are distinctly different.

Value? Okay, there's the catch. How much does it really do for me?

"YOU NEVER GET A SECOND CHANCE TO MAKE A FIRST IMPRESSION"

- Get the Highest Price for Your Home. A well-staged home is aesthetically pleasing. Everything looks inviting, comfortable, and simple. It elicits a strong emotion from buyers: desire.

- Your Home Will Sell Faster – The Association of Property Scene Designers states that staged homes sell for 43% more quickly than unstaged homes.

- Staging Helps with Procrastination – yes, your stager will want many of your collector items put away. This is called de-cluttering and depersonalizing. You will have to tackle this at some point. Get it done early, store boxes in the basement, a POD, or rent a storage unit for a few months.

- Staging will teach you a Few Things. Maybe you never had a decorator and you've done it all yourself. Those floral curtains in the bedroom, the layout of the pictures over the living room sofa, the furniture placement in the family room or the overlarge chair in the den. It all works for you which is great – but a stager might just show you "better" which is something you can take with you to your new home.

- You Never Get a Second Chance to Make a First Impression – is a favorite line with stagers and real estate agents. If you don't stage before you list, guess what? You've lost time and money – the two things that are all but promised if you stage your home before listing it for sale.

- You get a good feeling when you walk into a home that has been properly staged. It's not fake, it's more than just place mats and wine glasses on the dining room table. It just feels good.

Sara Golden

DESIGN YOUR KITCHEN LIKE A MILLENNIAL

*by **Maxwell Alexander***

Ah, Millennials, it warms my heart writing about Us – the most consciously awaken generation humans produced so far. We literally design the world around us in sync with Nature and the Universe. So what does it means to design a kitchen like a Millennial?

KITCHEN IS THE NEW LIVING ROOM

Millennials are awakening to the wisdom of the Cosmic Intelligence and taking into account the experience of the previous generations, they realize that anything related to food is crucial to our existence, not only because of the physical nourishment and wellbeing but also as a spiritual connection with our innate nature and other human beings. Sitting around a fire pit while preparing and sharing food, socializing, creating stories and memories is where life happened for our ancestors who were a lot closely connected to Nature. Millennials spend a great deal of their time not only socializing, but also working in coffee shops recreating the ancient environment and conditions where humans operate most efficiently while feeling their best. Now that Millennials are finally ready to build their own nests, and knowing that they will spend most of their time with the family cooking organic meals and socializing in the fully equipped kitchen, they bring the coffee shop concept with them. Walls are crumbling, dining rooms are being torn down – Millenials are hard at work making the open floor plan a reality.

Whew! The era of plastics is officially over! Thank you, but no thank you, Babyboomers! We are back to basics and embracing wood, steel, concrete, and natural stone. Walls, floors, furniture, and appliances are things we touch and in the air, we breathe, so why should it emit toxic fumes in the space where we spend most of our time? Plus, the use of sustainable materials like wood proactively protects the climate and serves as a repository of carbon emissions. Millennials are ditching their mom's plastic countertops and replacing them with simple, environmentally-friendly and cost-efficient concrete or quartz counters.

Millennial way or not, it's a great time to rethink your kitchen design. **Duncan Avenue Design Studio** is Hudson Valley's leading interior design agency and in collaboration with **Tough Construct | Hudson Valley**, they can execute a jaw-dropping overhaul of your kitchen space.

Visit ToughConstruct.com to learn more.

What you won't find in the Millennial's kitchen/living/dining space is a TV. Fortunately, Millennials hadn't had a chance to get hooked on the whole "cable" idea, whatever entertainment they need to get is at everyone's fingertips, so there is no reason to cover all the beautiful natural concrete/stucco walls with obnoxious plastic panels. In the meantime, a chalkboard is a great alternative to digital overload, so why not make an entire wall as a billboard for family-wide announcements, recipe display or a point of creative collaboration!

MILLENNIALS ARE BACK TO BASICS WHEN IT COMES TO CHOOSING INTERIOR MATERIALS

INDUSTRIAL AUTHENTIC RUSTIC

CLASSY INDUSTRIAL LOOK, MODERN RUSTIC STYLE

Modern Rustic, Industrial Style is hot, especially with Millennials who appreciate reusing and recycling while staying classy and sophisticated. If you squint your eyes in Millennial's kitchen, you'll see a lot of grey-ish, brown-ish, black-ish and whitish colors reflecting in natural light. Remember the caves we lived in generations ago? I bet you'd see the same picture if you squint your eyes in one of those. Industrial shelving solutions are so in and you still got a chance to find a great deal at a nearby scrap metal place or a flea market. Hit garage sales this weekend for unique and environmentally conscious furniture. Dig into your grandma's attic for one of a kind decor for your Millennials-inspired kitchen.

FENG SHUI, YING YANG, BALANCE...

Wellness is about balance and Millennials take both very seriously. Whether you are a fan of centuries-old feng shui traditions, understand why Ying can't survive without Yang, or just following a common sense and balanced approach, you'd know that too much of good could be just as bad. Balance is the key, especially in kitchen design. Space should flow naturally, with enough square footage to breathe. Entrance to the kitchen should be either wide or cleared of any obstructions. Having storage in the kitchen is essential, however, try to hide unappealing items in cabinets below eye level and balance shelving with clear wall space ("white space" in layout design). If you use feng shui practice to decorate your home, you know the power of plants. Plants attract good energy. They also absorb negative energy and distractions. Surround yourself, neatly, with large smooth-leaved plants in earthenware pots. The plants and pottery represent the mountains and create supportive energy. Two good plant choices are the golden pothos and areca palm.

SCIENTIFICALLY JUSTIFIED & CULTURALLY EMBRACED SMART LIGHTING DESIGN

Lighting is a crucial element in interior design and if you are spending most of your time in your kitchen/living/dining/socializing space, you should know the facts. Lighting is like a lens that reveals the reality around us, and if the lens has an incorrect prescription, it will sure to give you a headache and affect your health negatively. Millennials are the smartest generation in the history of human civilization, they dictate the new lighting design trends:

An abundance of natural light is the best way to go. Our bodies are designed to thrive in the natural light, so it's important to welcome it inside the kitchen space.
LED Edison bulbs use a lot less energy and generate warmer light frequencies that create a cozy and stress-free ambiance.
Oversized industrial light fixtures are trendy and great at preventing the artificial light sources shine directly into your eyes and guide the light rays where they are needed.

WHO IS YOUR BUYER?

[MILLENNIALS]

36%

[THE LARGEST MARKET SHARE]

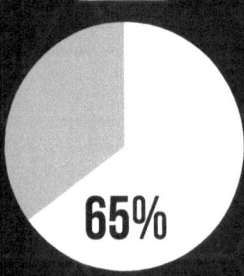 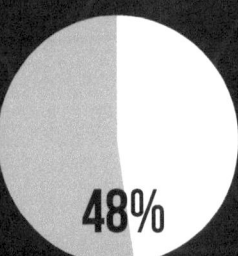 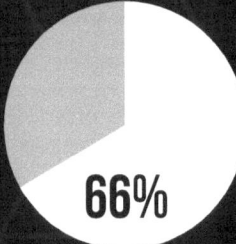 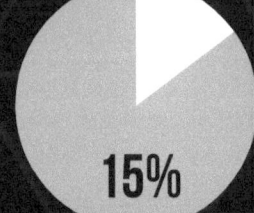

65%
FIRST-TIME HOME BUYERS

48%
HAVE CHILDREN

66%
MARRIED COUPLES

15%
UNMARRIED COUPLES

 GENERATION X
38 - 52 Y/O

26%
[OF ALL HOMEBUYERS]

$104,700
[MEDIAN INCOME]

MOST LIKELY TO BE MARRIED & MOST LIKELY TO HAVE CHILDREN

[MOST RACIALLY & ETHNICALLY DIVERSE]

26%

IDENTIFYING THEY ARE A RACE **OTHER THAN WHITE/CAUCASIAN**

BUY THE LARGEST HOMES IN MEDIAN SQFT.

PURCHASE THE HIGHEST MEDIAN PRICED HOMES

[YOUNGER BABY BOOMERS]
53-62 Y/O

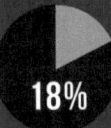 **18%**

[OLDER BABY BOOMERS]
63-71 Y/O

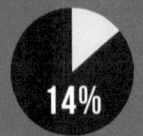 **14%**

[THE SILENT GENERATION]
72-92 Y/O

 **6%**

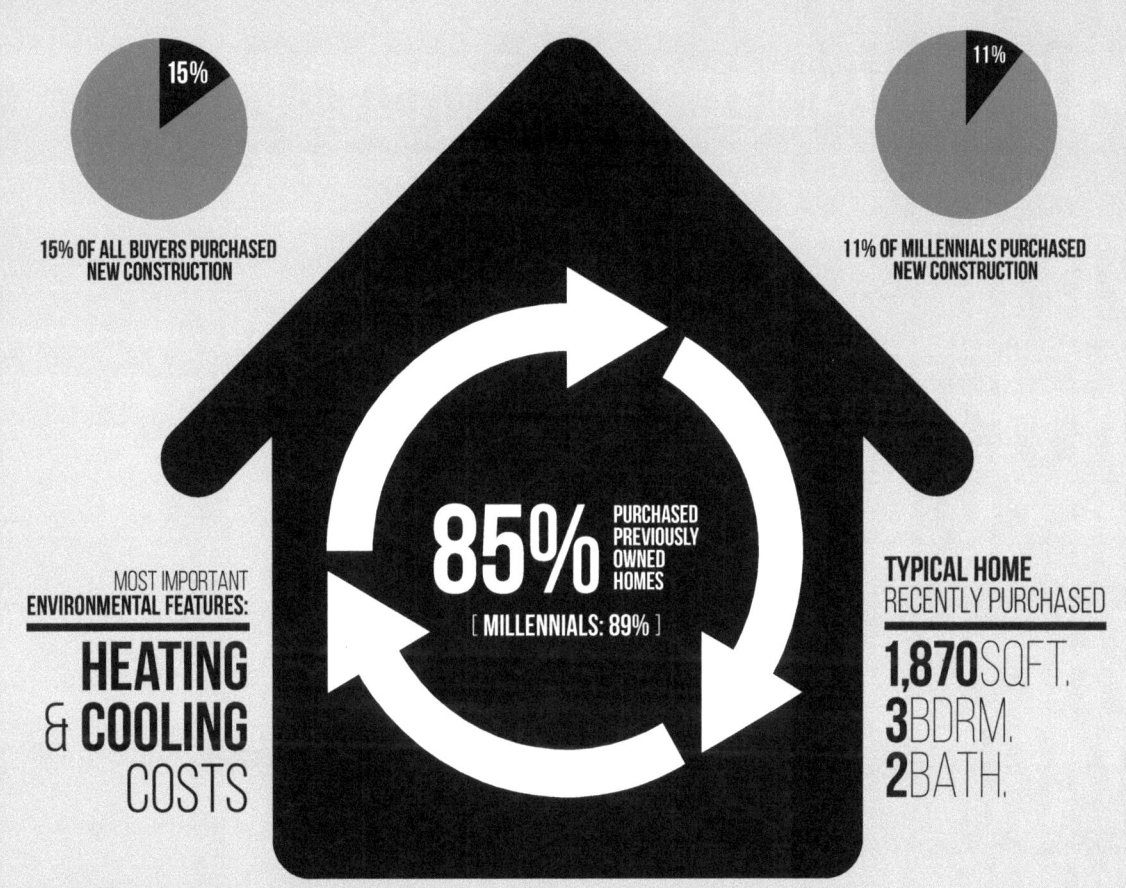

15% OF ALL BUYERS PURCHASED NEW CONSTRUCTION

11% OF MILLENNIALS PURCHASED NEW CONSTRUCTION

MOST IMPORTANT **ENVIRONMENTAL FEATURES:**

HEATING
& COOLING
COSTS

85% PURCHASED PREVIOUSLY OWNED HOMES

[**MILLENNIALS: 89%**]

TYPICAL HOME RECENTLY PURCHASED

1,870SQFT.
3BDRM.
2BATH.

90%

90% OF BUYERS UNDER AGE OF 62 CONSIDER **PHOTOGRAPHY** AS THE MOST IMPORTANT FEATURE WHEN SEARCHING ONLINE

DATA SOURCE: 2018 HOME BUYER AND SELLER GENERATIONAL TRENDS REPORT BY **THE NATIONAL ASSOCIATION OF REALTORS®**

AM ALEXANDER™ MAXWELL REALTY

SELLING YOUR PROPERTY?
ASK US ABOUT **COMPLIMENTARY** ALL-INCLUSIVE
STRATEGIC MARKETING PACKAGE

LOG ON TO **ALMAXREALTY.COM** & JOIN US ON INSTAGRAM! @ALMAXREALTY

[PRESENTED BY **ALMAXREALTY.COM**]

2019 INTERIOR DESIGN TREND: BARN DOORS

Barn doors are no longer an outdoor feature, but a stylish yet rustic Hudson Valley Style interior design trend. Known for their functionality and space-saving features, they are in high demand among ToughConstruct clients in Hudson Valley's Cornwall on Hudson, New Windsor, Newburgh, Wallkill, Goshen, Pine Bush, and Beacon areas. With the help of ToughConstruct (2018 Hudson Valley Style, Design & Sustainability Awards Winner), discover why adding a barn door is an ideal home improvement project that will bring modern rustic style into your home.

BARN DOORS ARE A PERFECT ELEMENT TO CONNECT ROOMS WITHIN AN OPEN FLOORPLAN

BARN DOORS ARE A PERFECT CONVERSATION PIECE

Interior doors are not just art hanging on the wall, but also serves an important function, they also can showcase a homeowner's style and personality. Barn

CUSTOM BARN DOORS ARE TRENDY YET CLASSY

Just like a piece of clothing, home decor often goes out of style, however, barn doors have been around for centuries and are an essential part of the Authentic Hudson Valley Style. Many Hudson Valley homeowners go with a modern, sophisticated look, rustic wood look or with a chalkboard barn door that adds another layer of functionality in the kitchen or a kid's room.

Adding a custom-built barn door in your Hudson Valley home could dramatically

As open floor plans gain popularity among homeowners in the greater Hudson Valley region, interior doors are evolving as well. Barn doors are one of the most efficient yet trendy approaches to connect adjacent rooms into one open floorplan space.

"The organic modern rustic look of custom barn doors adds warmth and cosy feeling into an interior," says Designer Maxwell Alexander of Duncan Avenue Design Studio. "The space-saving flexibility of a barn door is an important function of adjusting and controlling interior environment to one's liking." Conventional hinge-mounted doors are out of fashion and take 2 times more space than a barn door that slides on a rolling track.

doors are a perfect conversation piece when entertaining family and friends. If your home is lacking a statement piece that inspires creativity and sparks conversation, contact ToughConstruct today to get a free quote for a custom-built barn door that will perfectly fit your space. Take a look at brand door examples of ToughConstruct's previous clients.

improve interior design of a space, not only from a visual perspective but also from a functional perspective. Imagine adding a few more square feet of space that doesn't have to overlap with a door rotating on hinges? High-quality, custom-built brand doors by Hudson Valley's best contractor will refresh your interiors and make you ready to meet one of the most beautiful seasons in the Hudson Valley!

STOP THE MOWING MADNESS WITH AN ECO-FRIENDLY LANDIDA™ ROCK LAWN

by Maxwell Alexander, CEO & Founder of Landida™ — Smart Landscapes

While a thick carpet of grass is, unfortunately, the most common lawn option, many homeowners in the United States and all around the World are drawn to the appeal of maintenance-free rock lawns. These pebble-based ground coverings are ideal for regions that are under watering restrictions due to drought (which is basically the entire Planet earth), or for homeowners who are just tired of constant mowing and inhaling pesticides/herbicides that come with their grass lawn. The installation process is similar to installing mulch or rock in a flower bed but encompasses the entire lawn instead. A rock lawn requires almost no ongoing maintenance and actually draws attention to the low-maintenance, evergreen shrubs and trees. In addition, Landida™ Smart Landscapes rock lawns look equally good in the winter as they do in the summer.

LANDIDA™ SMART LANDSCAPES / ROCK LAWN BENEFITS

Eliminating the grass from a lawn may seem like a drastic move, but it actually has many time saving and eco-friendly benefits.

- Reduces the amount of time required to mow, water and fertilize grass.

- Conserves water by eliminating the need to water the lawn.

- Reduces or completely eliminates pesticides applied to the lawn.

- Reduces the amount of yard waste, such as grass, leaves and pine needles, that is sent to the landfill.

- Some cities located in drought-prone areas of the Southwest even provide tax breaks for homeowners who replace their lawn with rock or gravel. This incentive strives to conserve as much water as possible for human consumption.

WHAT TO EXPECT WHEN INSTALLING LANDIDA™ SMART LANDSCAPES

We will measure the width and length of the lawn, and multiply the two numbers together to arrive at the square footage of the lawn. We will determine how many tons of rock you need by dividing the number by 100 for 1-inch diameter rock or by 110 for 1/2-inch diameter rock. These measurements are for the recommended installation depth of 2 inches.

AMERICA
IS CONVERTING TO **INTELLIGENT LANDSCAPES**

are **You?** *ready*

landida™
SMART LANDSCAPES

get grass-free at landida.com

LANDIDA™ PROFESSIONALS WILL PREPARE THE AREA

Landida™ Smart Landscapes experts will remove all grass and weeds from the area using a spade to slide under the top 1 to 2 inches of soil. We will place the material into a wheelbarrow and move it to a compost area preferably on your property or a certified compost site. We will not remove any trees or shrubs that you want to remain in place. Instead of spraying the ground with an herbicide, we will install black weed-barrier landscaping fabric.

INSTALLING THE LANDIDA™ ROCK LAWN

Landida™ Smart Landscapes Experts will spread the material out to an even 2-inch thickness using a bow rake. They will repeat the process of spreading out the rock until the entire surface of the lawn is covered. Although we can use any type of gravel or rock desired, river-run gravel is rounded and more comfortable to walk on for both humans and pets, and bluestone 3/8 gravel is just as comfortable to walk on plus has a stylish and sophisticated look. We will rinse the top of the rocks with a garden hose to remove any white residue.

No matter the motivation, Landida™ Smart Landscapes Rock Lawns are attractive landscaping options for all areas of the country. Not only do homeowners reduce the amount of money they spend on the lawn, they gain more time to enjoy their home instead of just maintaining it.

ENJOY YOUR YARD INSTEAD OF MOWING IT!

REAL ESTATE **PHOTOGRAPHY 101**

61%
MORE VIEWS ONLINE
WITH PROFESSIONAL PHOTOS

UP TO ●●●●
47%
HIGHER ASKING PRICE/SQFT

80%
OF BUYERS
CITED THEY WOULDN'T EVEN CONSIDER A LISTING WITHOUT PHOTOGRAPHS

98%
OF BUYERS
THINK PROFESSIONAL PHOTOS ARE MOST USEFUL WHEN LOOKING FOR HOME ONLINE

AERIAL & DRONE IMAGING

CONSIDER THESE HIGH-TECH UPGRADES

PROFESSIONAL LIGHTING

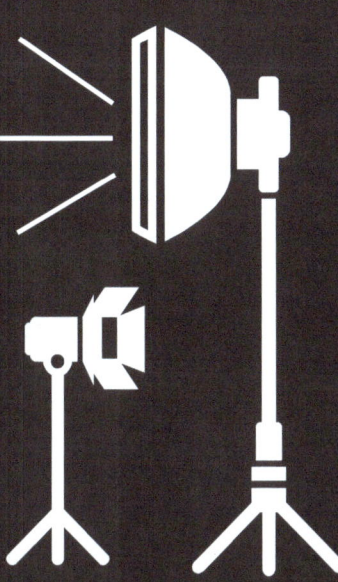

DSLR CAMERAS & LENSES

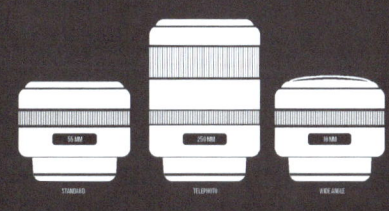

PROFESSIONAL RETOUCHING

+ DIGITAL STAGING

[LET THERE BE... LIGHT!

Photo Story
by **Maxwell Alexander**

DUNCAN AVENUE'S
VILLA 9W

Copper Leaf / Architectural Light Panels →

Materials ↓

← Black Hardware

↑ Paint Colors

← *Stainless Steel Backsplash*

ENTERTAINING IN STYLE

A Pop of Green ↓

← Stainless Steel
Appliances

↑ Copper Leaf Pendant

↑ Concrete
Floors

Quartz Countertops ↓

[HUDSON VALLEY STYLE LIVING]

← *Custom Copper Lights*
© *Duncan Avenue Design*

White Granite Wall →

Wood Accents →

← *Formal Dining Area*

LIVING | WHITE
BALANCE

Custom Entertainment
↓ Console

[HUDSON VALLEY STYLE LIVING]

EXPERIENCE THE MAGIC OF HUDSON VALLEY™

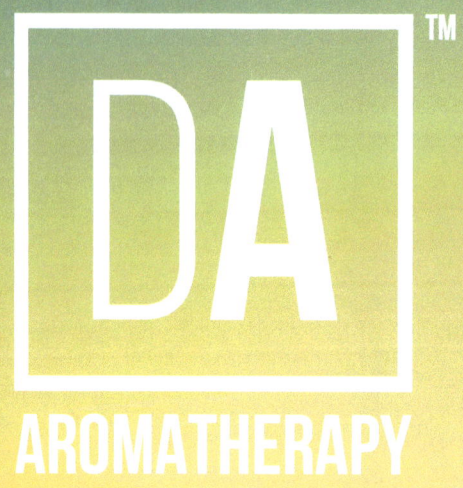

AROMATHERAPY

PLANT DERIVED INGREDIENTS / NO PARABENS
NO SULFATES / NO DEA/MEA VOC-FREE / BIODEGRADABLE
CRUELTY-FREE / GOOD FOR YOU & GOOD FOR
THE ENVIRONMENT / MADE IN THE USA / DESIGNED &
CRAFTED IN HUDSON VALLEY

DA-AROMATHERAPY.COM

NATURAL HAND SANITIZERS WITH ORGANIC ESSENTIAL OILS

by DA Aromatherapy Collection

Working out at the gym or taking a Savasana on your yoga mat? Protect yourself and loved ones plus get an aromatherapy boost on the go with these natural hand sanitizers.

DA Aromatherapy Hand Sanitizing Mists with Organic Essential Oils are effective against 99.9% of common germs and bacteria.

DA-AROMATHERAPY.COM

$9.00

WOODLAND TRAILS BLEND

by DA Aromatherapy Collection

This natural insect repellent is made with 7 organic essential oils, it provides broad-spectrum protection and repels mosquitoes and ticks, fleas and many other pesky insects. The Best Natural Tick and Mosquito Repellent Spray is created for direct skin contact, safe for Humans and Pets and featuring exclusive Woodland Trails™ blend of Organic Lemongrass, Eucalyptus Lemon, and Eucalyptus Globulus, Cedarwood (Cedar Oil), Rosemary, Clove, and Lavender Essential Oils.

Our signature Tick and Mosquito Natural Spray will keep you sting and bite-free without the use of pesticides that are harmful to humans, the environment at large and especially good insects like honeybees. Our natural tick and mosquito repellent can help to protect you when sprayed in a room, on the balcony, in a car, on the body, and even on your clothes without staining.

DA-AROMATHERAPY.COM

$17.00

INSPIRING AROMATHERAPY MIST WITH ORGANIC LAVENDER AND SANDALWOOD ESSENTIAL OILS - WINDS OF STORMKING™

by DA Aromatherapy Collection

A luxurious and sensual fragrance of rich, woodsy sandalwood accord and beautiful flowery notes of lavender and spice. Winds of Stormking™ Essential Oil Blend perfectly captures the cool mountain breezes, sun sparkles in the Hudson River waters and lush foliage of the Hudson Valley.

DA-AROMATHERAPY.COM

$9.00

FIND YOUR HOME

#ALMAXREALTY
#HUDSONVALLEY
#REALESTATE

AM ALEXANDER™ MAXWELL **REALTY** | EQUAL HOUSING OPPORTUNITY

ALMAXREALTY.COM // 845-518-2750
309 WALL ST, SUITE 1, KINGSTON, NY 12401
N.Y.S. LIC.# 10491207973

#PLANTSCAPING IS AN ALL YEAR ROUND ENTERPRISE

[PLANTSCAPING TIPS BY DESIGNER **MAXWELL ALEXANDER**]

Plants are a powerful but underused tool in interior design. Their green, leafy bodies can add life to even the coldest rooms and they are versatile enough to be able to be included either as a major feature or as a last minute detail. But as living creatures they are, plants can be tricky to work with since they need good lighting, settings, and the right planters to look their best. So make sure you keep these tips in mind to breathe style and nature into your home's interior.

PLANTERS ARE MORE THAN JUST CONTAINERS

Plants and planters go together like two peas in a pod. Rather than just being containers, planters can make a statement of their own and add personality to a room by varying in shape and size according to a particular theme. When picking a pot's color, it's always a good idea to look at the surrounding objects palette to guarantee it fits into the design.

USE DIFFERENT LEAF TEXTURES AND SHAPES TO MAKE A STATEMENT

Rooms would look boring if every texture used in them were the same. You can avoid this by using bold leaf textures and shapes to break patterns and create an interesting mix of figures. For example, you can use high cascading plants to break the blocky look that tall pieces of furniture give to living and dining rooms. Likewise, you can also breathe personality onto empty corners or long walls using small, tree-like plants such as palms.

[HUDSON VALLEY STYLE INTERIOR DESIGN TIPS]

PLACEMENT CAN BE USED TO CHANNEL TRAFFIC OR ATTENTION IN A SPACE

When resting on the floor, plants can act as portable walls, helping to subdivide a room into more intimate spaces or simply channeling traffic through large areas. This is ideal for larger rooms, as it makes people comfortable and creates visual depth. Plants can also be used as frames to draw attention to a particular area or object, like a window or a door, by putting two identical ones on either side.

ROTATE BLOOMING PLANTS TO MAXIMIZE THEIR VISUAL IMPACT

Blooming plants, such as bromeliads and orchids, add an exotic touch to a home and bring a sense of life to even the darkest days. But with their average lifespan being six to eight weeks, you'll need a trusted source of blooming plants and frequent rotation to ensure your clients can enjoy their view year-round.

CHOSE THE RIGHT LEAF COLORS FOR YOUR PROJECT

Leaf colors can add variety and life to a room. When picking between colors, use them like a chef uses spices to add subtle flavors to his creations. You can go for the classic green-over-white look or vary your palette according to the season: green for spring, teal for autumn, etc. Color options are limitless and include many variations of green as well as more exotic ones like white, silver, purple, and orange.

USE SPOTLIGHTING TO HIGHLIGHT THE PLANTS

Don't let your plants blend with the rest of the props. Instead, use spotlights to bring attention to beautiful plants and accentuate their role in a room. Take advantage of their uniqueness as the only living pieces of décor in a home to create an aesthetical ambiance that is both natural and pleasant to the eye.

aglaïa

AERIAL PHOTOGRAPHY IN THE HUDSON RIVER VALLEY

*by **Maxwell Alexander***

Hudson Valley Homes and Estates really do have a lot of character, not to mention that the architecture, landscaping and nature setting is truly stunning. With the backdrop of the Hudson Valley, it is a prime location for aerial drone photography. With years of experience, it is safe to say that we work diligently to make sure that our clients get the result they want out of their aerial photography and this is especially the case if they are trying to sell or market their property. With breath-taking photographs and a friendly team who will work closely with you every single step of the way, you know that you can count on us to go that extra mile while also delivering remarkable and stylish photos that you never thought possible.

HARNESSING THE POWER & BEAUTY OF NATURE

We know that nature is truly a force to be reckoned with, but in the right situation, it can also provide you with the perfect setting for an inspiring photo shoot. It doesn't matter whether it is sunset, sunrise, in the middle of a heatwave or snowing like it's Christmas Day because we have the ability to use every situation to your advantage. This means that we capture photographs like you have never seen before and it also means that the end result won't be like every other real estate photography out there.

OUR TALENTED AND FRIENDLY TEAM

Led by Maxwell Alexander, World-Class Art Director and Photographer, our team knows exactly how to approach a luxury property with flawless execution. We take into account the style of the home, the surrounding greenery and more, before planning our angle of approach and camera view. This gives us the chance to capture your home in the best possible way while also giving us the chance to provide every single viewer (your potential buyer) with a unique and magical experience.

OUR DRONES AND PILOTS

When you come to us for all of your drone photography needs and requirements, you'll find that we have the latest professional equipment and only FAA-licensed drone pilots. Not only does this mean that we are able to deliver a better result than our competitors, but it also means that we have the experience you need to really stand out from the crowd.

OUR SPECTACULAR AERIAL REAL ESTATE PHOTOGRAPHY

Aerial Photography is one of the best ways to highlight your Real Estate Property including indoor and outdoor photo and video shots. We can cover landscape features and look and feel of the neighborhood, all of it is important to your potential buyers.

If you are interested in our team, how we can help you or even to see if there is anything that we can do for you then please do get in touch with us today. We would love to hear from you and we are very excited to work with you to get you the best result out of your aerial photography.

Review Our Aerial Photography Portfolio and Schedule Your Aerial Photo Shoot at DuncanAvenue.com

DA SKY™
AERIAL PHOTOGRAPHY
by
DUNCANAVENUE™
BANNERMANS ISLAND
ARSENAL
[DUNCANAVENUE.COM]

TO STAGE, OR NOT TO STAGE?

Learn More about this design project →
at duncanavenue.com/design

STAGED HOMES **SELL 79% FASTER**

STAGED HOMES SOLD **IN 11 DAYS OR LESS**
ON AVERAGE SPEND **73%** LESS TIME ON THE MARKET

COMPARED TO AVERAGE: 50 DAYS ON THE MARKET

81% OF BUYERS FIND THAT STAGING HELPS THEM BETTER **VISUALIZE A PROPERTY AS THEIR FUTURE HOME**

HIGHER SALES PRICES
STAGED HOMES **SELL FOR 17% MORE** THAN NON-STAGED HOMES

BUYERS MOST OFTEN **offer 1%-5%** increase on the **REAL VALUE** OF A STAGED HOME

SELLERS SPEND LESS THAN **1%** FOR STAGING SERVICES to get a **1000% RETURN ON INVESTMENT**

HOME STAGING CAN BOOST **PERCEIVED VALUE OF A HOME BY 20%**

95% OF BUYER'S AGENTS SAY THAT HOME STAGING HAS A POSITIVE EFFECT ON THE HOME BUYER'S VIEW OF THE PROPERTY

3% YET LESS THAN 3% OF HOMES LISTED ON MLS ARE STAGED

HAVING YOUR HOME PROFESSIONALLY PHOTOGRAPHED?

by **Maxwell Alexander,** President, Chief Design Officer, Duncan Avenue Group

The real estate market in the Hudson Valley and around the Globe has been changing rapidly, and that has created some challenges for home sellers. It was not that long ago that searching for a home meant driving from New York City all the way to beautiful Hudson Valley neighborhoods, picking up flyers and sales packets and maybe stumbling upon on open house or two.

In the 21st century, home searches are more likely to start online while at lunch break in the office than in the family car. The ease of browsing real estate listings online is hard to beat, and potential buyers can scour dozens of listings in the time it would take to visit just one in person.

The shift to online home shopping has created both challenges and opportunities. If you understand how home buyers shop and what they are looking for, then you can make your listing stand out and rise above the rest. If you fail to put your home in its best light, would-be buyers could pass your home by as they do their online shopping.

Hiring a local Hudson Valley professional photographer is one of the best ways to make your home stand out. Duncan Avenue Real Estate Photography Studio is your premier professional photography provider in the Hudson Valley area including Orange, Rockland, Dutchess, Ulster, Putnam, Westchester, Greene, Rensselaer, Columbia, Saratoga and Albany Counties. We'll take care of making your online photographs stand out, but there are certain things you should do before the pro arrives. Here are the steps you should take while you wait for the photographer.

SECURE YOUR PETS

If you have a dog that is aggressive, territorial or just protective, be sure to secure the animal long before the photographer is scheduled to arrive. We love dogs, and in fact we've got two super hyper Jack Russell Terriers at home, however they could definitely get in a way of making your home look good in the pictures, especially if they are so cute that it's just way too distracting.

Even if your pets are not too aggressive, they could get in the way during the photo shoot. Placing your cats and dogs in the basement or garage is a courtesy you should extend to the professional who will be photographing your home.

START A FIRE

If your home has a fireplace, we would want to show it off. Be sure you have a roaring fire going in each of your fireplaces before the

HERE IS WHAT TO DO BEFORE THE PHOTOGRAPHER ARRIVES

photographer arrives.

A lit fireplace will not only make your home look inviting, but it also serves as proof that it's working correctly. A fireplace can be a big selling point, so do not sell yourself short.

| LIGHT SOME CANDLES

You can create a homey and inviting environment even if your home does not have a fireplace. Just pick your favorite candles, scatter them around the house and light them up when the photographer arrives.

A set of tapers on the table will create a romantic setting and make your finished photographs look great. A large pillar candle in the living room will create an inviting atmosphere and encourage browsers to take a look. Use your imagination, and ask your Hudson Valley Real Estate Photography Pro for other lighting ideas when he arrives.

| LIGHT IT UP

Speaking of lighting, turn all the lights on before the photographer's scheduled arrival. If any light bulbs are burned out, take the time to replace them. Set the dimmers to full power so that your home looks as bright and airy as possible.

You can let even more light in by rolling up the blinds and opening up the curtains. You want the space to be as bright and inviting as possible, and that brightness will come through in the finished photographs.

We will bring supplemental lighting with us to make sure all areas of your home look the best they can.

| CLEAR OUT THE DRIVEWAY

We would want shots of the driveway, so remove any cars, trucks or other vehicles before the scheduled photo shoot. Be sure to park them well down the street, keeping the road in front

of your home open as possible. Duncan Avenue Photography Studio is the only Real Estate Photography Studio that offers complementary FAA-licensed aerial/drone photography with every property or listing package.

Staging your home for open houses and private showings is important, but making your home look great in the listing photographs may be even more important. You can think of your listing photographs as a special kind of staging, one designed to draw the eyes of would-be buyers and get them to schedule a private appointment.

Make your appointment today at DuncanAvenue.com